MICROSOFT OFFICE 365

YOUR GUIDE TO DIGITAL TRANSFORMATION WITH OFFICE 365

BEN TAYLOR

TABLE OF CONTENTS

CHAPTER ONE

MICROSOFT TEAMS

Microsoft Teams Getting Started with Teams and Channels in Microsoft Teams for Microsoft 365

Microsoft Teams provides users with an efficient collaboration feature to establish teams and channels which serve as fundamental elements for sharing and team communication. Microsoft Teams consists of project members who are called Teams yet Channels describe specific interest areas within a team structure.

Here is the process to establish teams together with channels through Microsoft Teams:

1. Setting up a Team

In Microsoft Teams a Team represents a fundamental concept that unites people together with their discussion threads and files along with their functional tools required for an objective or project completion. Within three primary team types Microsoft Teams functions as the primary workspace to exchange communication that supports departmental and project work and topic-based operations.

Microsoft Teams

Steps to Create a Team:

1. **Open Microsoft Teams**: Start Microsoft Teams Application or launch Teams on the web if the application has not been installed.
2. **Click on Teams**: Your Teams appear under the Teams section of the lefted sidebar on the website for selection.
3. **Create a New Team**:
   o The bottom section of the sidebar contains a Join or create a team button that users need to select first.
   o Click Create team.

4. **Choose a Team Type**:
    o **From Scratch**: Users can choose between Private, Public and Org-wide team options after selecting New team under From Scratch. All members added to the team by the system leadership will have access to private teams.
        ▪ **Private**: The system directly decides all membership in private teams.
        ▪ **Public**: The team membership extends to personnel at every operational level with Public teams because the organization allows any employee to join.
        ▪ **Org-wide**: Small organizations can enable Org-wide to add their entire membership to the team (too large organizations need to turn it off).
    o **From an Existing Group**: If you already possess an Office 365 group from Outlook or SharePoint the system allows team creation by selecting the create from an existing Office 365 group option tab.

5. **Name Your Team**: Your team needs a basic name that suits its purpose either as Marketing Team or Product Development team or Customer Support Team.

6. **Add a Description**: The addition of a team description would let members understand its main purpose when you choose to create one.

7. **Set Privacy Settings**: You must choose between team privacy options for the team because going private will allow select members only while going public will welcome all organizational members to join the team.

8. **Add Members**: Joining your team requires two options for members: they can provide their email address or perform a search among workplace users.

9. **Click Create**: After finishing your settings choose the Create button to generate your new team.

2. Setting up Channels

Within a team that collaborates on one project various topics will require their own separate discussions called channels which exist physically. Teams possess numerous channels that enable administrators to divide discussions so each topic stays distinct.

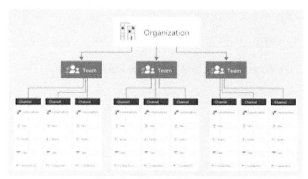

Setting up Channels

Types of Channels:

- **Standard Channels**: The standard channels in a team provide open availability for all team members through standard messaging features.

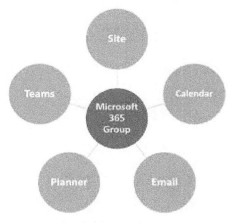

Standard Channels

- **Private Channels**: serve specific purposes because they limit access to particular workers who need to talk to one another in large teams.

Private Channels

Steps to Create a Channel:

1. **Select Your Team**: You can reach the Teams tab to select the team where you want to create your new channel.
2. **Click on More Options (Three Dots)**: Click on the three dots situated in the right portion of team names because this will reveal a menu dropdown.
3. **Select Add Channel**: Choose Add Channel by selecting it from the available drop-down choices.

4. **Name Your Channel**:
   o Pick a clear descriptive title when creating channels which describes what they contain (such as "Product Launch," "Our Marketing Strategy," "Team Messages").
   o The name should be accessible to everyone who participates on the team.
5. **Set Channel Privacy**: Choose between:
   o **Standard**: This channel permits universal participation by every member who belongs to the team.
   o **Private**: This channel allows access to chosen team members whom you need to select from a list.
6. **Add a Channel Description**: Channel members should understand its main functions through an explicatory description which appears inside the channel.
7. **Automatically Show this Channel**: Through Automatically Show this Channel members can manage whether this channel appears in the open channel list for all team members.

8. **Click Add**: Press the Add button when all modifications to the channels are ready to create them.

3. Channel Settings and Management

Your created channels will allow you to modify settings and make changes until they meet your work group requirements.

Managing Channel Settings:

1. **Edit Channel Settings**:
   - For name or description or privacy changes in a channel navigate to the right side of channel name then press the three dots (ellipsis) to open an Edit Channel option.

2. **Manage Permissions**:
   - **Who Can Post:** The ability to post messages in the channel operates through two permission settings: allowing anyone to post and restricting it to owners.
   - Channel administrators can modify permission settings under Manage Channel > General > Who Can Post through the selection offered within the available list.

3. **Channel Notifications**:
   o Through the alert notification setting users have the ability to track all channel activities from individual channels. Select your notification options among All Activity, Mentions, and No notification from the Channel Notifications interface.

4. **Delete a Channel**:
   o Right click on a channel to access the Channel List where you should select the option to Delete Channel. Creating a channel leads to permanent deletion of all content found inside the channel during the process of deletion.

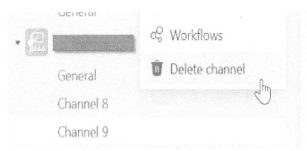

Delete a Channel

4. Organizing and Collaborating in Teams and Channels

The following phase of management consists in building your teams and channels along with preserving their organization and unity.

Pin Important Channels:

- The user interface enables arranging channels through declaring preferred channels for a prioritized front position. Right-clicking the channel name allows users to pin it by selecting the Pin option.

Pin Important Channels

Using Tabs for Quick Access:

- Users can create tabs from the channel to access files and applications as well as other services such as OneNote, Planner and sharp team.

14

o You need to navigate to the upper part of your channel then use the + symbol to generate a new tab with important tools.

Messaging and Sharing Files:

- **Post Messages**: Create discussion by posting messages either formatted for specific users by tagging with the@ symbol or by adding message reactions.
- **Share Files**: The direct file upload in the channel enables users to co-edit documents at the same time as users can also share links to their resources through this feature.

Using Channel Conversations:

- The messages flow through channels which contain separate threads for conversation. The creation of new topics exists alongside answering previously posted messages to sustain conversation continuity.
- Replying with the click of the button under a particular message will group all related conversations together.

5. Managing Team Membership

Your task will include team member additions as Owners or Members while removing some members completely from your team structure.

Managing Team Membership

Add or Remove Members:

- **Add Members**: You can invite team members by clicking the work team name followed by the three horizontal dots to access Add Member which enables you to add people to these teams.

- **Remove Members**: You can remove team members through the manage team button followed by selecting the members tab to find options that let you remove members by clicking the X button under their name.

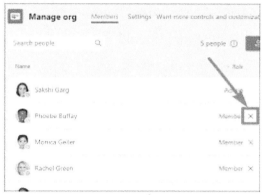

Remove Members

Assign Roles:

- **Owners**: Team owners enjoy full control of their Microsoft Teams platform by which they can modify individual member access settings as well as team settings.
- **Members**: Members in the team can contribute through posting news and commenting on other posts along with document sharing but they lack permission to update or adjust forum settings.

6. Use of Teams and Channels for Organizational Structures

Focusing on these practices will help maintain both organizational structure and operational effectiveness for your teams and channels:

1. **Clear Team and Channel Names**: Teams along with channels should receive names which explain their topic clearly to avoid ambiguity ('Marketing Team - Social Media Campaign' represents one example).

2. **Limit Channel Creation**: The continuing creation of new channels should be limited because it is not helpful at a particular time. Businesses should start with basic channels first before creating new channels according to organizational requirements.

3. **Use Private Channels for Sensitive Information**: Private channels represent the solution for maintaining confidentiality as you can shift specific discussions into restricted member spaces.

4. **Communicate Expectations**: Establish clear channel objectives together with usage criteria to help all participants learn channel management strategies.

5. **Regular Cleanup**: Regular cleanup involves reviewing every channel to determine whether they need archiving for future needs or whether they need elimination when their purpose is complete so you obtain more productive space.

Conclusion

Teams in Microsoft Teams require proper setup since they provide employees in necessary groups with essential tools that enable smooth cooperation. A proper execution of the described process enables workers to develop system-based work environments which boost team productivity levels.

Instant Messaging and Conferencing in Microsoft Teams (Microsoft 365)

Microsoft Teams serves as a platform that enables better teamwork through integrated communication functions which include message exchange and phone calls as well as document-sharing capabilities. The collaborative platform of Teams enables users to share messages regardless of their physical location whether they are in the same facility or from different districts that join. A description of the Microsoft Teams chat and collaboration function will display their applications for this purpose.

1. Chat Features included in Microsoft Teams

Users can find the basic communication feature Chat at the heart of Microsoft Teams where teams and individuals maintain real-time information sharing and coordination.

Types of Chats in Teams:

- **One-on-One Chat**: Users can conduct real-time communication with one person directly through this method without involving intermediaries.
- **Group Chat**: A conversation between several persons. Microsoft Teams allows users to build small group chats for specific teams or projects as well as add additional members to these limited circles.
- **Chat within Teams**: Team members who would join a Teams chat have access to view and add information to shared discussions.

How to Start a Chat:

1. **Open Microsoft Teams**: Begin by launching Microsoft Teams under the Chat function and proceed to the Launch Teams interface.

2. **New Chat**: New Chat begins by clicking on the pen icon paired with the paper sheet icon that you will find at the top of your screen.

3. **Add People**: In the To field, enter the name of the person or a group you want to talk with.

4. **Type Your Message**: The text box located at the bottom of the window enables you to send your message by typing. The message sending process allows users to include emojis and attach files to their discussion with others.

5. **Send Message**: You can start a message transmission by pressing Enter from the device's keyboard.

Chat Features:

- **Rich Text Formatting**: Chat users enjoy various options to normalize their messages through bold text as well as italics lists together with colored formatting. The toolbar located beneath the message box holds this feature.

- **Attach Files**: The paper clip icon on the toolbar lets you share computer files within OneDrive or other linked applications.

- **Mention People**: Tagging people directly for mention occurs by using the '@' symbol followed by their name inside a conversation window within the chat interface.
- **Replying to Messages**: The reply feature initiates intra-conversation interactions by using the Over icon when clicking on any message post.
- **React to Messages**: The fast way to acknowledge messages through emoji reactions includes using the thumbs up or the heart symbols.

2. Collaboration in Channels

A specific group obtains its communication and collaboration through channels which represent individual sub-websites within Teams. Project teams find channels beneficial to conduct project-related discussions with colleagues who have sharing interests. Channels also enable discussion of overall topics that need review.

How to Start Collaboration in a Channel:

1. **Navigate to Teams**: Open Teams through the left frame by selecting Desk Teams followed by picking the team channel for your work.

2. **Post a Message**: Creating new posts through Posts tab requires you to type your message then press Enter for starting a conversation.

3. **Share Files**: Apart from providing the attached files icon at the screen's bottom users can share files by selecting that icon within the channel's interface. Inside the channel users have the option to add files through their interface buttons. The Files section of a channel opens all uploaded files by default.

4. **Use @Mentions**: You can use the @Mention function to attract attention because it allows targeting individual users through specific mentions or the entire team distribution.

Best Practices for Channel Collaboration:

- **Organize Conversations**: Each channel contains too much information so team members can use threads as an organizational tool.

- **Pin Important Posts**: Important files and messages within a particular channel should be pinned for easy access through the feature which allows users to position them at the top of their corresponding channel. The pin option can be found by right-clicking a message.

- **Keep Messages Clear and Focused**: Maintain messages with lucid statements to stop confusion from unclear information which needs unified agreement from team members.
- **Use Channel Tabs**: The sharing and collaboration of files and OneNote as well as Planner or other applications should occur through dedicated working tabs in each channel. Users can add tabs through a button positioned at the upper section of the channel.

3. Real time Collaboration between people on a document

Teams allows users to work simultaneously on documents that remain saved in Microsoft 365 through OneDrive and SharePoint and their various office applications.

Collaborating on Office Documents (Word, Excel, PowerPoint):

1. **Open the File**: To begin working you need to pick any document from the files tab in a channel panel.
2. **Edit Together**: Several team members can jointly edit this document through the Edit Together feature. Microsoft provides each user with their own

24

colored cursor to show who makes which document edits.

3. **Chat while Editing**: Users can perform real-time chat operations through the Chat pane while editing documents to maintain editing dialogue. The functionality allows users to maintain contextual communication so they avoid returning to Teams.

4. **Track Changes and Comments**: The Track Changes feature of Office apps enables users to place notations and questions directly in the document text.

5. **Version History**: The Version History function enables unlimited document edits as well as modifications to content with replacement options for any past version that needs recovery. Open File > Info > Version History to check previous document versions and choose from one of these versions for restoration through the restore option.

4. Video and Audio Calls for Collaboration

Video and voice call options within Teams enable teams to handle all forms of real-time work collaboration including group meetings as well as employee-to-employee discussions.

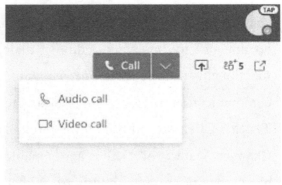

Video and Audio Calls

How to Start a Call:

1. **From Chat**: To start a video or voice call launch Chat and click on the video or voice symbols facing right in the page corner.
2. **From a Channel**: Users can begin meets from channels through this process: Point the cursor at a channel beneath the Posts tab then select Meet Now from the top right of that screen.
3. **During a Meeting**: A specific meeting enables you to activate either your camera or microphone to communicate with your team members.

Video and Audio Call Features:

- **Screen Sharing**: Users can switch active application sharing through Screen Sharing features that enable them to showcase their current work with other participants.

- **Virtual Backgrounds**: Teams lets users modify their video call background with Virtual Background options either for work scenarios or silly moods.

- **Recording**: The system lets you record calls through which recorded calls end up in the Files tab of meeting chat for later usage.

- **Live Captions**: Teams offers live captions as a feature to provide audio transcription during teams meetings for users who have hearing difficulties.

5. Group Collaboration Features

Teams provide multiple features which support group work in a joint environment:

Team-Wide Announcements:

- The Format button located below the boxes offers Announcement as a selection for any chosen channel. Hard-coded announcements receive additional emphasis through both the bar element positioned above the frame and bigger color selections.

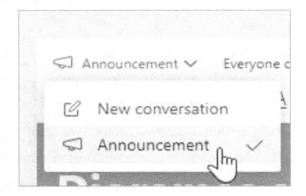

Planner for Task Management:

- Within the Teams Planner application members can receive assigned tasks through setting tasks to monitor their performance. Users can place a Planner tab for task management anywhere inside their selected channels.

Polls and Surveys:

- Microsoft Forms provides Teams users with an in-app feature to make new polls directly from their interface. Teams offer a polling system which serves perfectly to collect feedback or group decisions among team members. Users can create a poll by accessing the Forms app available in the message composer according to their instructions.

Polls and Surveys

Whiteboard for Brainstorming:

- Whiteboard allows Teams users to attach drawing features for collaborative note writing sessions through pencil tools and shared note participation during meetings. Whiteboard presents a useful tool for sharing ideas with colleagues since everyone can monitor workstation activities collectively.

6. Notifications and mentions for Cooperation

Notifications together with mentions along with activity alerts provide team members real-time updates without missing out on key team developments.

How Mentions Work:

- Users can tag specific colleagues with a mention using @ whereas the @team directive tags all members within the chosen group. The notification system ensures proper person-to-person notification delivery.
- Messages documents and meetings contain features that enable you to mention specific team members.

Managing Notifications:

1. Access your profile picture by clicking on the top right section of the main Flicker page.
2. You can find Notifications under the Settings application by scrolling to that screen.
3. Modify settings for messaging receive and mention notifications together with monitoring your team's activities within the platform.

7. Using Guest Access when Working with Other Teams

Teams provide users an option to work with external participants (guests) who include customers along with business partners or vendors. The platform permits users to view channels and take screenshots and access channels as well as meetings and file sharing capabilities.

Adding a Guest:

1. **Add a Guest to Your Team**: I access Teams where I find our designated team followed by selecting the three dots beside the team name then choosing Manage Team from the options.

2. **Invite a Guest**: I can add new guests by accessing the Members tab where the Add member button can be found to enter their email address before hitting the Add button.

3. **Set Permissions**: The ability to configure permissions in the system rests on your choice whether the guest user can generate messages or see files.

Conclusion

Microsoft Teams stands as a complete software that features extensive chat and collaboration capabilities which enhance organizational teamwork by enabling info sharing and project work between people and groups. Everything necessary for group communication exists in the Teams platform in which workers can stay in constant contact and continue their work. The various features including task management and polls and file sharing with guest access enable Teams to simplify collaboration no matter where team members work.

Video Calls and Meetings in Microsoft Teams (Microsoft 365)

Users benefit from multiple video call and meeting Facilitates in Microsoft Teams to work alongside others in real-time. Regardless of needing to talk with one person or conduct a group meeting with colleagues Teams provides all essential communication tools.

1. Learn how to schedule a meeting in Microsoft Teams

You can create a meeting through Teams by accessing the platform with desktop application or mobile application or outlook. One can set a meeting time through the scheduling feature to determine when meetings should take place and manage participant invitations.

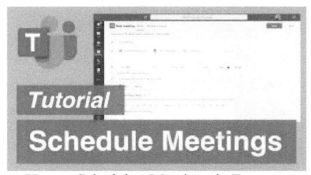

How to Schedule a Meeting via Teams

How to Schedule a Meeting via Teams:

1. **Open Microsoft Teams**: Users need to activate Microsoft Teams either through the app start or by accessing the web platform.

2. **Go to the Calendar**: Use the Calendar component by lowering the left sidebar and choosing the calender-shaped Icon.

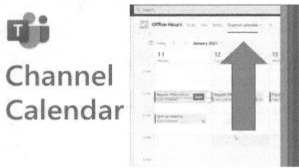

Channel Calendar

3. **New Meeting**: Users must open 'New Meeting' from the top-right corner area of the screen.

4. **Set Meeting Details**:
   - **Title**: Create a simple title that will make the meeting identification easy for all participants.
   - **Attendees**: The event attendees section requires a list of attendee email addresses

either for invitation purposes or to let them view the event. Your meeting distribution can take place within your organization's personnel along with external speakers as guest participants.

- o **Date and Time**: should represent the meeting length spanning from beginning time to finish time. The typing option allows you to specify when to display the meeting while another choice permits scheduling it for a different point in time.

- o **Meeting Location**: The location for the gathering requires inclusion when physical meetings take place. For virtual meetings the option is to keep this section empty or provide a link to Microsoft Teams.

- o **Description**: Both objectives and preparatory context can be integrated under the "Description" section to assist participants.

5. **Choose a Channel (Optional)**: Users who want to schedule meetings within specific channels can choose the desired option from the available list.

The selected channel allows all its members to join meetings because of this functionality.

6. **Send Invitation**: You should click Send to dispatch invitations to everyone registered for the meeting after making all necessary account entries.

Scheduling a Meeting via Outlook:

- Start by opening the Outlook application then navigate to the "New" section in your calendar.
- Select your meeting details and pick the Teams Meeting suggestion while adding Team link.
- The summary of the meeting can be sent with the invitation through a click of the button.

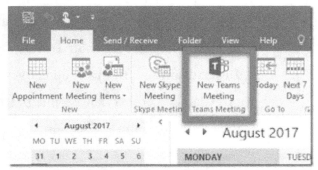

Schedule a Microsoft Teams

2. Joining a Meeting

The participants receive their meeting link by accessing the calendar invite sent to them by schedule. You can create

Microsoft Teams meetings by using the scheduling system accessible through Teams and Outlook and also from meeting invitations that provide a link to join.

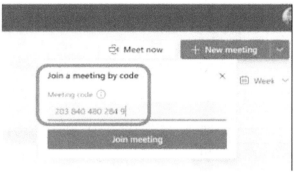

Joining a Meeting

How to Join a Meeting:

1. **Join from Calendar**:
   - Navigate through to the Calendar in Team.
   - The scheduled meeting appears under the Calendar section so users should press 'join' to access the session.
   - When the meeting time comes, Click Join.

2. **Join from a Meeting Invite**:
   - The Join Microsoft Teams session appears when you click the link provided through email or calendar invitation.

- o The user interface allows a selection between Desktop app and Browser to join meetings.
- o Users must select their joining method between Desktop application and Browser interface.

3. **Join via Mobile App**:
- o On your mobile, run the Teams app.
- o Users must select the Calendar option followed by selecting the corresponding meeting.
- o Click next to the join button to enter the meeting.

3. During a Meeting

Participants engaging in Teams video meetings have access to multiple tools for better decision-making throughout their meetings.

Meeting Controls:

1. **Mute/Unmute Microphone**:
- o Background noises can be muted through the microphone control which becomes

available with one click on its icon. Click again to unmute.

Mute/Unmute Microphone

2. **Turn Camera On/Off**:
   - Users who wish to stop video recording can disable the camera function by clicking at the camera icon. The interface automatically disables the feature after period yet enables the options when pressing the same button again to proceed.

Turn Camera On/Off

3. **Share Screen**:

   - The Share Content button located at the top toolbar has an upward arrow overlaid on a square which enables you to distribute content.

   - The mode allows users to choose between entirely showing their computer screen or specific working windows and PowerPoint presentation windows.

4. **Use Background Effects**:

   - While participating in a meeting users can utilize virtual backgrounds to activate ON/F Off settings or feed blurring functions for maintaining privacy and forming formal meeting settings.

   - Open the background settings in Microsoft Teams by pressing the three horizontal dot (ellipse) then select Apply background effects to view background options.

5. **Chat During a Meeting**:

   - A meeting participant can type comments or ideas through the Chat function which allows access from the preparatory panel during active sessions. The Chat icon will activate the message window for typing messages.

- Users have two interaction methods through @Mentions which specifically alert designated participants in the chat.

6. **Reactions**:

- Emoji reactions enable you to react to conversations by using the check, clapping or heart symbols. The tool benefits users by showing interest through supporting evidence while staying focused on the discussion.

7. **Record a Meeting**:

- Users can start recording meetings by clicking the '...' function in the Meeting controls section followed by selecting Start recording. The recording function in Microsoft Teams saves the meeting data to both the chat area and file section thus enabling retrieval any time.

- The recording formats available for meetings include audio type and video type as well as sharing screen type.

Record a Meeting

4. Breakout Rooms

The Breakout Rooms function serves meetings containing numerous participants who require structured discussions between specific groups of two to four members. More than five participants can use this feature within Team meetings.

Breakout Rooms

Setting Up Breakout Rooms:

1. **Start a Meeting**: New meeting creation begins in an empty Teams space where you join your team members before making the appointment.

42

2. **Create Breakout Rooms**:
   - Integration of Breakout Rooms appears when a meeting reaches more than six participants through the controls function.
   - The number of swimming pool rooms must be determined before starting the architectural process.

3. **Assign Participants**:
   - The program has two options to distribute participants through random assignment which lets the system decide or user selection by picking names from the central display.

4. **Start Breakout Sessions**: Rooms open through pressing the Start rooms button for breakout sessions. The program transfers participants to different assigned areas according to their assignment.

5. **Return to Main Session**: The host role enables you to access any session that was created as breakout rooms. The session ends when you select Close Rooms which will send all participants back to the primary gathering.

5. Meeting Features for Larger Teams

Teams supplies specific features for large meetings that enable participants to connect with each other as well as machine systems.

Live Events:

- Teams Live Events delivers exceptional performance for meetings and broadcasts that require one or several speakers to engage their audience.
- Users can determine event attendees while simultaneously managing guest questions along with running polls through Q&A.
- The feature serves webinars and company conferences together with similar large meetings.

Live Events

Meeting Options:

- Users can control many meeting features such as letting participants skip the lobby and setting initial silent status for new participants and choosing video permissions.
- You need to access the Meeting Options during scheduling or during a running meeting in order to modify these settings.

6. Post-Meeting Activities

Teams provides two fundamental features to maintain and follow up meetings that already took place.

Meeting Recap:

- Human life ends by performing the final automatic meeting summary just before the session concludes. Participants receive meeting notes from their attendees together with recorded conversations and voice messages provided the feature was activated. The summary of the meeting exists in two sections: Files and the meeting chat.

Tasks and Follow-Ups:

- Planning and assigning out highlighted tasks from meetings should be done through the combination of Tasks by Planner and To Do applications.
- The participant has two options for responding to sent emails: they can create additional notes in the OneNote meeting tab or directly send a reply through email.

7. Meeting Security and Privacy

The platform implements security protocols at the enterprise level which safeguards the privacy and confidentiality of meeting participants and all shared contents from unauthorized access.

Meeting Security and Privacy

Meeting Security Features:

1. **Lobby**: You can make a lobby where players is in a waiting until the host admit them playing.

2. **Who Can Present**: For this session, other people will not be able to present to everyone as presenting are limited to specific person only.

3. **End Meeting for All**: The host of the meeting itself and himself or herself can end the meeting to save themselves as well as everyone else from time wasting in meeting.

4. **Recording Consent**: Those participating in it will receive a notification that a consent for recording of a specific meeting is required and without consent, no recording can be done.

8. Meeting Best Practices

To run more effective and effective meetings, here are some best practices:

1. **Prepare and Set an Agenda**: Bring the participants up to speed with the issues discussed using an agenda, to stay away from any shocks and establish a focus on discussion.

2. **Test Equipment**: You should speak into your mic, turn on your cam and check that the screen sharing is working before joining the meeting to avoid any potential snags.

3. **Mute When Not Speaking**: For background noise, mute on some part of your PC with loud noise during non speaking.

4. **Engage Participants**: When you are presenting, engage the participants by the use of Polls, Q&A and Reactions.

5. **Use Meeting Notes**: Action the decisions and tasks made during the meeting or minute taking the meeting or OneNote for detailed minutes of the meeting.

Conclusion

Microsoft Teams is one of the most widely used platforms for video calls and conferences at large, incorporates everything required to work successful by remote mode. Whether it is an ordinary dialogue, business-cal or high-level conversation, it connects team had and it also works. This makes Teams to provide a lot of features that allow for well-structured and secure meetings in a seamless manner; some of the features of it includes Screen sharing and Breakout rooms sharing, live events, Meeting recording.

CHAPTER TWO

ONEDRIVE FOR BUSINESS

Microsoft 365: Saving Files in OneDrive and SharePoint

Microsoft 365 is giving efficient, cloud Storage NT solutions to store manage share files. Microsoft provides cloud storage tools, inclding that peoples can access any time to their files and work along any with it and also the option is inclding for protect the data. In Microsoft 365, it are the two main services provided for cloud file storage are OneDrive and SharePoint, that concentrate in different areas in file usage.

1. OneDrive for Personal File Storage

OneDrive is the cloud service storage what was developed to the sake of one user. It allows users to get to files anywhere there is internet from practically world making with item suitable for particular use to store, back-up and confirm files.

Key Features of OneDrive:

- **Personal Storage**: The user creates a portion of the project or local storage for files, for which the project can be run through any device PC laptop, Mobile etc.

- **Syncing**: In OneDrive information can be sync or back to multiple devises. No connection to the internet is required for operation and you only synchronize the changes when you are back online.
- **File Sharing**: Share is easy where you could send to other via contact or even via Teams portal just clicking the link. It is possible to give permissions to edit or just to read and even share files to anyone not belonging to the team.
- **File Versioning**: OneDrive has intrinsic feature that it stores version history files. This allows you to return to the original copy with your practice on the questions.
- **Integration with Microsoft Apps**: Of course, OneDrive is compatible with Microsoft Office applications including Word, Excel, PowerPoint. You can also work with Word, Power Point, Excel or PDF dockets within OneDrive in a similar way to SharePoint without having to download them initially.
- **Security**: Files in OneDrive are secure as it's sent across and also when saved to service because it is

encrypted. Also there are precautions to take such as two-factor authentication (2FA) that helps secure your identity.

How to Store Files in OneDrive:

1. **Upload Files via the Web**:
   - o Visit the OneDrive website from the Internet, using the one of the following browsers:
   - o When running with free ssh you can single click on Upload in the top menu and drag/drop files or folders that you want to upload.

Upload Files via the Web

2. **Using OneDrive Desktop App**:

   o Once you open the OneDrive web application, you will have to download and also run OneDrive on your computer.

   o Files to be moved to the OneDrive folder on the computer. These files will behave just like the older files that you became familiar in Lesson 1, sync to the cloud.

Using OneDrive Desktop App

3. **From Office Applications**:

   o Remember to save from application as Word, Excel and PowerPoint document to store directly file in the could one drive.

2. Use of SharePoint for the Purpose of Storing and Sharing Team Files

SharePoint is actually designed for communications and collaboration for an organization's team of contributors. It permits enhancing the centralised file and document storage and sharing around an organisation with a specified methodologies destiny access right alone, process and appropriate communication. It's great for working as a team if you are working with documents of any kind or one of the team members has need to share this particular file particularly for your project with your someone else.

Key Features of SharePoint:

- **Team Sites**: There are ways to build cooperative areas in Teams through SharePoint – such as Team Site, where the team can store documents, track activities, and manage resources.
- **File Versioning**: Just like OneDrive, SharePoint allows tracking of the version history of the file so a

user can view last version, restore or compare with the ones.

- **Permissions Management**: With NTFS you can define particular rights for users or groups, in this way you can establish whether a folder and/or a file can be requested, written or removed.
- **Document Libraries**: Documents can be kept in a library where documents can be stored, shared and managed in a central repository.
- **Co-Authoring**: It can be edited by other people too while you are editing and all the changes are instant.
- **Workflows and Automation**: As one of the SharePoint features, users can set up the task that incorporates the ability to obtain document approval, inform others or alternatively are transferring data within certain workflows.

How to Store Files in SharePoint:

1. **Create a Document Library**:
   - To do this, go to the Team Site in SharePoint or, if you do not have it, create a new site in the application.

- There is possibility to build a Document Library for documents categorization and sharing with members.

Document Library

2. **Upload Files**:
   - From a document library, to add filings or ascertain whole file folders from your computer, then click 'Upload'.

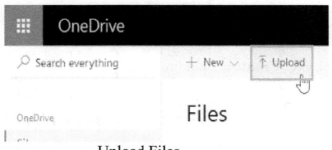

Upload Files

3. **Sync SharePoint to Your Computer**:
   o The OneDrive sync app is the app to use when synchronizing Libraries in SharePoint to the desktop. Especially, it allows local access to file for edit, then to upload modified file to cloud after you are connected to internet.

4. **Collaborate in Real-Time**:
   o Words, excel and power-point you can edit only in a Real time – how many people at the same time edit file. The Toolbar has the particular feature called Version History where you can see the entire edits.

3. Comparing OneDrive and SharePoint

FEATURE	ONEDRIVE	SHAREPOINT
Storage	Individual storage per user	Centralized storage for teams and departments
Primary Use	Personal file storage and sharing	Team and organization-wide collaboration
File Sharing	Share with	Share with teams or

	individuals or groups	specific groups with custom permissions
Collaboration	Basic collaboration (for personal files)	Advanced collaboration (teams, projects, workflows)
Permissions	Set file-level permissions	Set site and library-level permissions
Syncing	Sync files to personal devices	Sync files to team members' devices
Document Management	Personal use with limited document management	Advanced document management with workflows, versioning, and permissions

4. Managing and Organizing Files

With the good organization of the files in OneDrive and SharePoint there is efficient sharing and access when required.

OneDrive File Organization:

- **Folders**: Albums are classified with subdivisions by making folders. For example you can have head such as, project-related, client or departmental sub folders.
- **Tags**: Tags are also used in file organization as it can be used to search files that are specific duration.
- **Shared Files**: When the files are shared among others they will be placed within Shared folder.

SharePoint File Organization:

- **Document Libraries**: categorize them depending on team. project or the theme and make multiple counts of it.
- **Metadata and Tags**: Organize documents by properties (metadata or tags) including file type, status or project.
- **Views**: The final feature is related to displaying files in various views depending on the project, date or status.

5. File Security and Compliance

Both OneDrive and SharePoint enable you to work securely and have various security features to prevent unauthorized access to your data.

OneDrive Security Features:

- **Data Encryption**: Data security is protected because of how the files are encrypted both.
- **Two-Factor Authentication (2FA)**: It also, provides another security feature to your account.
- **File Sharing Permissions**: Shared file can only be viewed or it can be edited as per your decision.
- **Activity Tracking**: Activity monitoring enables the monitoring of everybody who wishes your files, and have edited them.

SharePoint Security Features:

- **Granular Permissions**: You can set permissions as per site, Document Library, Folder, Document levels when you use SharePoint.
- **Compliance**: Office SharePoint integrates with Microsoft 365 compliance options like IRM, Discovery and DLP.

- **Audit Logs**: SharePoint provides administrators to monitor People, their activity and file access in the SharePoint site on the basis of audit logs for enforcing compliance and security requirements.

6. Accessing Files Anywhere

The strongest benefit of saving files in OneDrive and SharePoint in the cloud format is ability to access them from anywhere and anytime.

Access from Desktop:

- OneDrive or SharePoint sync app makes it possible to synchronize files down to the computer, and they can be accessed even when there is no internet available.

Access from Mobile:

- You can synchronize the Office documents on all your devices in order to be able to edit them and distribute them wherever you go: install the OneDrive or SharePoint at smartphone or tablet to work with the files.

Access via Web:

- This implies that so long as you have signed up for an account with Microsoft OneDrive or Sharepoint, then you can access your files via the internet from your browser you do not need to put in any additional software.

7. Interaction with Other External Open University Consumers

As it is mentioned earlier, the collaboration with the users in OneDrive is possible as you can invite users from outside your organization along with One drive to share files to them.

External Sharing in OneDrive:

- Send the contents to people beyond your firm by granting the recipients access to the shared file via a Web link.
- You have the option to allow / not allow to view or edit of the files to the outside users and the option when the sharing link expires.

External Sharing in SharePoint:

- SharePoint sites allow external users to join internal collaboration efforts with organization partners so they can co-own files which users can work together on in the same site.

- SharePoint owner needs to set permissions to external users either for reading content only or enabling both reading and writing access.

- Different roles operate at different levels because admins both permit external users' access and deny external access to others.

Conclusion

Everyone and every group receives exceptional convenience together with security along with integrated teamwork tools when files are saved in the cloud through OneDrive and SharePoint. The application OneDrive suits individual requirements for file sharing but SharePoint functions mostly to enable team collaboration and corporate file management. Microsoft 365 suite components integrate both tools to provide users with a seamless experience for work activities and secure document sharing alongside efficient protection. Storage in Microsoft 365 provides benefits to users who work independently and those who collaborate together at all times.

Files options in MS 365 (OneDrive and SharePoint)

Microsoft 365 includes share and synchronization tools that enable users to connect files across multiple devices and synchronize them with co-workers for strongly enhanced collaboration. From One drive and SharePoint users can distribute individual documents and folders as well as complete libraries throughout all system platforms. Review the following links to learn about file sharing and synchronization in One Drive and SharePoint Microsoft 365 applications:

1. Sharing Files in Microsoft 365
Sharing Files from OneDrive

Users of OneDrive maintain the functionality to distribute files and folders among team members and external people including internal organizational teams.

Sharing Files from OneDrive

How to Share Files in OneDrive:

1. **Open OneDrive**:

   o Open either onedrive.com through your computer browser or launch the OneDrive application from your colorful device.

Open OneDrive

2. **Select the File or Folder**:
   o You can choose to select or right-click a file or folder after which you can click on the icon containing three dots in the file's context.
3. **Click on "Share"**:
   o Choose the option that says Click Share.

Click on "Share"

4. **Choose Sharing Options**:
   o **People in your organization:** A default share to anyone within your organizational structure exists when posting files in the organization dashboard.
   o **Specific people**: Disclose to those special persons, both internal and external to the

organization. The sharing process requests the input of email addresses from receivers which you can present using this structure You will need to input their email address.

- o **Anyone with the link**: All users holding a link to the content will have access to view it without requiring any login information.
- o **Can edit / Can view**: The system will next determine whether recipients should view the file only or possess editing permissions.
- o **Expiration Date / Password Protection**: The link security features include a password option and expiration duration which help protect your content.

5. **Send the Link**:
- o Users need to input a message before clicking send to distribute the file or folder to recipients.
- o The link shows two options for its sharing action where recipients can duplicate the link to send through different channels.

Sharing Files from SharePoint

The main purpose of Microsoft SharePoint serves as a collaboration platform where users can distribute company documents as well as company libraries or organized folders.

How to Share Files in SharePoint:
1. **Open SharePoint**:
   o To over the change to your SharePoint site and navigate into the library that contains the particular document of your choice.
2. **Select the File or Folder**:
   o To share file or the folder, you just have to tick the checkbox into that area concerning these elements.
3. **Click "Share"**:
   o From the toolbar you will have to go to Share or right click the mouse and from the appeared menu – click more dots.
4. **Choose Permissions**:
   o **Specific People**: Choose with whom you would like to share your moment.
   o **Anyone with the link**: It is okay for anybody who has the link to view the document, information or data put on the internet.
   o **Internal Users**: A forward to other members of the organisation.

- o **Can edit / Can view**: Here you have to choose whether they will have the option of editing the particular document or just viewing the document on the portal.

5. **Send the Link**:

- o If you want to add an optional message after that, to send the message, you click the button 'Send' or if you have the intend to share the message through other channels, you can click the button 'Copy Link'.

Send the Link

2. Files for Sync in Microsoft 365

Syncing Files with OneDrive

It offers one a convenient way of transferring files from one device to another or even updating an original file from any device. This environment is most appropriate for clients who shall prefer the offline environment and only update online.

How to Sync Files with OneDrive:

1. **Download the OneDrive App:**

   o Ensure that one drive application is well installed on the personal computer or one's mobile phone. If not, it can be downloaded from the official page of OneDrive in Microsoft.

Download the OneDrive App

2. **Sign in to OneDrive**:

　　○　To open OneDrive, start the application and if the user is in the environment of Microsoft Office, sign in with an MS or the account from the MS 365 suites.

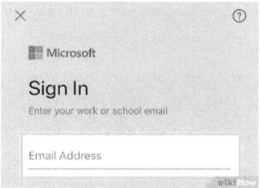

Sign into OneDrive

3. **Choose Folders to Sync**:

　　○　The first one allows you to select the certain folders for syncing in the OneDrive app while the second one can be applied when you want all your OneDrive.

4. **Sync Files Automatically**:

　　○　If you are using OneDrive program in your PC, every file and folder stored in any of the OneDrive folders will be synchronised. You create documents in the cloud storage and the same will be reflected in the storage of your computer.

o Files will be marked with a check to the left when the application is in the final phase and completely synchronized. That is why files that are not in Yahoo drive anymore have cloud icon on them.

Automatically Sync

5. **Access Files Offline**:

o As it can be observed, the advantages of synced files is that after a process of synching, the files may be retrieved though without the internet. In this case when you log into the internet again the changes made will be updated back to one drive automatically.

72

Syncing Files with SharePoint

Other features of SharePoint include document libraries which can also be synchronized with the computer so that one can work with them while they are offline and then come and upload them to the SharePoint.

How to Sync Files with SharePoint:

1. **Navigate to Your SharePoint Site**:
    - Go to the SharePoint site where your Document Library is located and then to the Document Library that you would wish to synchronize.

Navigate to Your SharePoint Site

2. **Click on "Sync"**:
    - When on the toolbar of the document library, click on the "Sync" button. This will open OneDrive sync client for you.

3. **Confirm Sync Setup**:
   - o In case if the dialog box is opened, to help the sync client to work with the documents, click on Allow. In case you are not logged in into MS Office then you can be asked to provide your Microsoft 365 sign in info.
4. **Sync Files**:
   - o The fields that are selected for synchronization are the contents of SharePoint in your OneDrive app on your PC. But now it became possible to reach these files and perform the manipulations with them, being offline.
   - o These will be seen again copying back to SharePoint once you connect again on the internet.
5. **Access Files from File Explorer**:
   - o It should be stored in the SharePoint folder and look like local files and available when Selected in windows file explorer or finder in mac os.

3. Users can synchronize files in multiple devices.

Some of the features of the OneDrive and SharePoint of One Drive are: using files across the PC, mobile phone and or tablets and sharing files in a real time manner while working.

- **Mobile Access**: There is a OneDrive application and/or SharePoint application on the iOS and android for use. It is used for uploading as well as sharing files and syncing them on an as required basis.
- **Web Access**: This links are easily accessed through the internet using the web addresses onedrive.com or sharepoint.com.
- **Multiple Device Syncing**: In this way, whenever I have files on my desktop – they are also in OneDrive or SharePoint on the other devices that I own.

4. Managing Shared Files and Permissions

That is why the files located in OneDrive and SharePoint enable identifying who can access a particular file and what can be done with it. It will also enable you to also always dictate and control the sharing of permissions that you set; specifically a certain project.

Shared Files

Managing Sharing Permissions in OneDrive:

1. **Go to Shared Files**:
   - For you to view the folder that has been shared you should open the OneDrive and click on the Shared where all the shared files will be depicted.

2. **Manage Access**:
   - If the Windows operating system is employed, right click on the preferred file or folder, you will then get a dot or the elipsis. He chooses the share and permission tab in order to modify or restrict them.

3. **Stop Sharing**:
   - Another option that can be found in the Manage Access section is the ability to stop

sharing of the file thus removing your share completely.

Stop Sharing

Managing Sharing Permissions in SharePoint:

1. **Go to Document Library or File**:
   - To perform the following steps, it's mandatory to get to the desired place in SharePoint: Go to either the Document Library or particular file location that you should work with.

2. **Click on the Ellipsis (three dots)**:
   - To unmount the device You right-click the file or folder and at the bottom other symbol (three points).

3. **Click "Manage Access"**:
   o Customers need to go to Access and set who can view the file, who can write on the file or their privileges of access.

4. **Remove Access**:
   o In the case of revoking access to users, you type the users name then click the delete button.

5. Best Practices for Sharing and Syncing Files

- **Use Links Instead of Attachments**: no large letters should be attached to the emails instead, share the recipients a link in OneDrive or SharePoint. This minimizes space and at the same time makes it convenient to utilize only the latest version and this would be always updated.

- **Control Access Levels**: When making the files and folders available to the other users through share option, it is advisable to grant them the least privileges that is view or edit privileges.

- **Regularly Review Shared Files**: It is also important to look at the files shared on that regard to ensure that the right people have access as well as delete any people who should not be accessing the file anymore.

78

- **Sync Regularly**: It is important that there are arrangements that if one has to work offline then the files are updated always on the gadgets. This is useful in preventing conflict that may arise when one is modifying elements on the same device.
- **Use Version History**: One should always retain the version history of an article where one can always retrieve the previous copies that contain the corrections made in case there was abuse made.

Conclusion

Working on OneDrive or SharePoint makes it possible to share documents with other co-workers as well as increases their security and convenience when used as tools of Microsoft 365. OneDrive is also preferred in the storage and sharing of files and documents as compared to the SharePoint that is more relevant to a group work. Two of them help you to move files within and outside the organization, to share the files, as well as to synchronize the files for one share access as well as to access the updated version of a file. Microsoft 365 provides efficient cloud storages to share as well as to synchronize files to enhance productivity and safe collaboration.

Microsoft 365 OneDrive and SharePoint to help you Organise your Files

Structure helps the cooperation and productivity in Microsoft 365; filing is an important factor that needs to be addressed. On the use of onedrive for personal file storage and use of share point in documents, there are realities why file management will be smooth, collaboration will be rewarding, and security will be boosted.

1. Organizing Files and Folders

a. Use Descriptive Folder Names: The structure of folders should reflect the group work and preference of work teams so as to make the location of a particular file easy to identify. For instance, instead of having a folder labeled as Docs, make it Marketing Reports 2024 to have a better perception of what the folder contains.

b. Create a Logical Folder Hierarchy: You should group your folders according to the department functioning in your organization or the projects undertaken or based on the document type to make it more distinguishable to the members of a certain department/team. For example:

- **Marketing → Campaigns → Campaign A → Reports of 2024**
- **Finance → Invoices → Client Invoices**

This thereby dislocates the free space to one wherein it does not experience by also making it easier to locate especial files.

c. Use Subfolders for Specific Categories: Use subfolders created into a large folder in order not to get confused with different files. For instance, suppose there is a Campaigns folder and some of its subfolders may be named as, for instance, Digital Ads Folder, Email Campaigns Folder and the like.

2. Naming Conventions

a. Be Consistent with Naming: Also, ensure that one makes as many subdirectories as should be as subdirectories, it is more important that there is standard approach to how files are named. It is therefore advisable to stick to the cleanness and standardization of text formats such as:

- Project_Name_Date_Version such as ClientX_Proposal_2024_v1.
- This reduces confusion when arranging the files and all employees are to comply with the certain procedure.

b. Use Dates in Filenames: To enable proper sorting of materials in the chronological order, run the filename by a date in the format of YYYY-MM-DD. This is essential, for instance, each and every time you are dealing with a new version or having repetitive reports.

c. Avoid Special Characters: Special Characters should not be incorporated into the file names as this would act as a disadvantage when syncing or sharing files * , / or any other symbol. Also, it is important to note that only alphabet characters, numbers, hyphens and underscores are permissible in the name.

3. Version Control

a. Use Version History: Both OneDrive and SharePoint provide the feature of viewing as well as restore previous version of the file. Use this element to observe changes in the shared document, preserve against erasing large amounts of information and get a duplicate of the completed work.

- **How to Enable Version History**:
    - ○ **OneDrive**: Right click on the file → Version history to view/ restore prior versions.
    - ○ **SharePoint**: Document library → three horizontal dots on the top right corner → Version history.

b. Manage Versions in SharePoint: Depending on the scale of the team, there is an option to set up the rules for versioning. There are three essential parameters to configure in relation to how many versions should be kept and when a new one should be generated automatically for the document.

4. File Sharing Best Practices

a. Use Links, Not Attachments: One should write shorts more covered rather than using the documents and file attachments every time. They ensure that any person who is given a link, can always download the latest version of a file and not some cached or outdated version.

b. Set Permissions Wisely: Access permissions should also be properly worked out while file sharing:

- **Can Edit**: Select this for collaborators which might require the permission to edit or make changes in their opinion.
- **Can View**: Select this for when you want to only provide viewing access to the document only.
- **Restrict External Sharing**: Do not share data to those outside your organization whenever the data is sensitive.

c. Use Expiration Dates: More often than not, when sharing files with outsiders involvement of links is made; use of links should however come with an expiry date. This helps in preventing additional cuts and expansion of safety features that make the files unavailable at some time.

5. Keep Files Clean and Updated

a. Regularly Review Files and Folders: It is good to always review the stored files and paper works during the weekends and also, it is essential to take time and remove any unnecessary papers that are there and also get time to organize the files that you have in a right manner. This is very important by creating some space on the disk by deleting some files that may not be useful at the moment and for all computer users, to construct organized storage space.

b. Archive Older Files: The files which are very large and are not used very frequently should be moved to the Archive folder. This creates bunching in an active work directory which makes it convenient for the current projects to be done.

c. Avoid Duplicate Files: There is also the need to avoid the occurrence of duplicity of copies in the storage system. In OneDrive or SharePoint, you can search for any copy documents which needs to be deleted, using the search bar. First, duplicates waste disk space both on your computer and external storage media; secondly, it is nearly impossible to determine which copy of a file is the most current among the numerous duplicates.

Duplicate Files

6. Cloud Storage Management

a. Sync Files for Easy Access: One is working with OneDrive and SharePoint files on the local computing device where there are two; the first method is synchronization. When you reconnected to the online system, documents will be updated afterwards. It is always important to make copies of documents and files to other devices in a bid to ensure they do not become obsolete.

- In OneDrive, to update the files one has to open the folder or the document, then using the computer mouse, click on it then choose Synch in the either the application or in web browser.
- For Share point, it then used the sync feature in order to help in synchronizing the team libraries across the devices.

b. Check Storage Usage: observe the usage of the cloud storage on OneDrive and SharePoint often so that one is not constrained by the storage space. Pay particular attention to the number of files you have and eliminating any file, which seems irrelevant.

7. Exploit Metadata and Tags (In SharePoint)

a. Add Metadata to Files: Metadata and Tags have been adopted at the National Office and in a research project at the University of Alberta as effective technical tools to enhance communication and the flow of information within workgroups and project teams.

b. Create Views Based on Metadata: Another point that needs to be made is that in the given platform, documents can be tagged to ease sorts or searches among them. For instance, through labeling like 'Q1 Report' or 'Confidential', one is able to look up the file and get an index of it.

8. File Security and Compliance

a. Enable Two-Factor Authentication (2FA): You should learn about enabling Two-Factor Authentication (2FA) as a security improvement measure for your Microsoft 365 account through Turn On Two-Factor Authentication (2FA) instructions. Using this method benefits the system through both data protection features and system access resistance.

2 Factor
Authentication on
OneDrive

Two-Factor Authentication (2FA)

b. Set Up Data Loss Prevention (DLP): Data Loss Prevention (DLP) policies in SharePoint and OneDrive should be intensified for better sensitive data protection. The DLP rules system acts to find protected data then protects the leakage of data that occurs through mistaken actions.

Data Loss Prevention (DLP)

c. Encrypt Sensitive Files: Deployment of encryption for sensitive files requires activation through Microsoft 365 features. Data stored in OneDrive and SharePoint travels through an encrypted connection by default and gets stored locked down in the same manner but administrators maintain control for implementing detailed encryption methods on sensitive files.

9. Automating File Management

a. Use Power Automate for Workflows: Microsoft Power Automate workflows in Workflows service allows users to manage their regular duties effectively. The system will transfer files to a specified folder based on specific criteria through automated processes that move files into the archive directory every 6 months.

b. Automate Alerts: SharePoint lacks an essential feature which enables users to obtain notifications about changes in OneDrive and SharePoint files. The feature enables you to monitor all updates while they happen instead of experiencing significant missed notifications.

10. Search and Find Files Quickly

a. Use Advanced Search: The features work identically for OneDrive as they do for SharePoint since these tools share a search service power that enhances measured discovery speeds along with general document accessibility. The advanced search capability lets you track down files using specific terms along with file formats or dates and tag labels.

b. Pin Important Files: The Windows application behavior of pinning files and folders also exists in OneDrive where anchorable documents and folders appear first in your file listing. Additionally you can utilize

SharePoint Follow to monitor your most accessed site locations and relevant documents.

Conclusion

The article shows proper usage of Microsoft 365 OneDrive and SharePoint to achieve order in your files and enable teamwork with fast document access. Through the implementation of these steps your organization can control its document storage alongside access and distribution practices alongside enhancing operational efficiency and enhancing document protection. The file management process enables smooth work practices and protects you from mistakes while providing access to current file updates.

CHAPTER THREE

SHAREPOINT

Creating and Managing Sites in Microsoft 365 (SharePoint)

The article shows proper usage of Microsoft 365 OneDrive and SharePoint to achieve order in your files and enable teamwork with fast document access. Through the implementation of these steps your organization can control its document storage alongside access and distribution practices alongside enhancing operational efficiency and enhancing document protection. The file management process enables smooth work practices and protects you from mistakes while providing access to current file updates.

Here are useful recommendations to build and manage SharePoint sites that boost teamwork and knowledge exchange while saving time.

1. Types of SharePoint Sites

At the beginning you should recognize the two basic SharePoint site categories:

- **Communication Sites**: Communication Sites do not work here since their core objective is to broadcast information to many people. A communication site serves to distribute public content like published newsletter materials and organization updates across the employee workforce and externally.

Communication Sites

- **Team Sites**: Team Sites exist for team collaboration allowing groups to exchange documents media schedules and action items. Team sites use Microsoft 365 Groups technology to combine better sharing between applications such as Outlook and planner.

2. Creating a SharePoint Site

Step 1: Access SharePoint

Start creating a SharePoint site by accessing your SharePoint platform.

1. Open Microsoft 365 in your browser and go to SharePoint either by clicking 'waffle' in the launcher or by going to sharepoint.com.

Creating a SharePoint Site

Step 2: Choose Site Type

1. To start a new site select the toolbar option Create site.
2. Choose between team and communication sites as your selection:
    - **Team Site**: Select Team Site when you are leading a team responsible for content translation.
    - **Communication Site**: The Communication Site enables you to send information to others in a shared online space.

Step 3: Configure the Site

- **Site Name**: Give your site an identifiable name (preferably an internal name, such as "Marketing Team Site" or "Company News").
- **Site Description**: Explain what the site aims to accomplish (Marketing campaign coordination).
- **Privacy Settings**:
    - **Public**: Non-team members from throughout your organization can view the site contents.
    - **Private**: While kept private the site lets only you create access for anyone you want.

- **Site Language**: When you launch your site choose its operating language here (the option can be altered later).

Step 4: Customize the Site

1. **Logo and Branding**: Your site identity needs a remarkable design element by integrating a distinct logo that customers should easily recognize.
2. **Home Page Layout**: Pick how Microsoft Office Picture, News, Quick links and Document libraries will display on your home page.
3. **Site Theme**: Choose your organization's design elements to match your brand identity.

Step 5: Create the Site

After entering relevant field information hit the Finish button. The system produces your new site and lets you continue modifying it.

3. Managing Site Permissions

The proper setup of site permissions in SharePoint helps maintain a system where authorized individuals gain access to create and access data. You can give permissions at both the site and its individual libraries folders and files levels.

Assigning Site Permissions

1. Click the gear icon in the upper right area of your SharePoint screen to open the settings.
2. Click Site permissions.
3. In the **Permissions** page, you can:
   - o To allow more users join the site click Add members. You can designate team members to three built-in roles like Owners, Members who manage permissions and Visitors who can see shared content.
   - o **Manage sharing options**: Determine exactly who can access the site by choosing from every user type including internal and external parties.

Granting Folder/File-Level Permissions

The system lets you block access to certain site sections:

1. Display the selected folder or file access using the left-click feature.

2. Right-click an item to open the menu then click the dots icon followed by Manage access.
3. Through manage access settings you can limit permissions from group or user inheritance and apply them instead.

Permission Levels

- **Owner**: An owner controls all aspects of the site including its content. The site owner can alter website configurations and permissions together with item updates.
- **Member**: The member can modify content while adding new files plus teaming up with others.
- **Visitor**: The visitor permission type lets users view files but they cannot edit them.
- **External Users**: External Users can access the site when you allow sharing and determine their sharing permissions.

4. Creating Common Web Parts and Web Part Pages for a SharePoint Site

A SharePoint site acts as your shared space to store and handle required content. These instructions show you the steps to add documents lists and content items to your site.

Adding Documents and Files

1. Visit your SharePoint site to access its Document Library section.
2. Click Upload on the screen and pick Files or Folder when you want to transfer documents from your PC.
3. Simply drop files from different programs into the document library.

Creating Lists

SharePoint Lists provide a method to handle organized information such as tasks, timelines, contacts and goods.

1. You need to start from the New option available on the site homepage to create a List.
2. Users can either select Issue Tracking template or use the Project Tasks list to establish a fresh list of their selection.
3. Use the provided window to choose the data type which can include text and date and choice options.

Create a list in SharePoint

Creating Libraries and Pages

- **Libraries**: Document libraries within SharePoint serve as repositories to organize documents properly. SharePoint supports multiple library creation for specific functions which include marketing document storage and financial document management.

- **Pages**: The system produces specific web pages to display content through organized systems. The development of your page requires only web parts including text components alongside images and document libraries along with news elements and others.

Create a Page

5. Customizing the SharePoint Site

SharePoint exhibits numerous customizing features which enable users to satisfy all individual company requirements. The platform enables users to schedule website content placements and put in optional web parts so they can customize their page.

Adding Web Parts to a Page

Web parts stands as solutions that enhance page functionalities in SharePoint platforms. Web parts enable users to show documents and news alongside calendars and various types of content through their website.

1. The Edit button enables page modifications when you navigate to the site you maintain.

2. The addition of new web parts begins when you click + Add a new web part to select from Document Library or App Picture or RSS Viewer or Content Editor or Html Entity Interpreter or Video priest or Recycle Bin:

   o **Document Library**: A document library or particular folder can either be displayed directly on the page by using this web part.

   o **Text**: content allows additional insertion through RTF and HTML formats.

   o **News**: The News section displays current developments as well as everything pertaining to the community.

   o **Quick Links**: Quick links need to contain direct access to vital documents alongside other sources that employees frequently need to reach.

   o **Image Gallery**: Showcase images.

Site Navigation

Users should have no difficulty moving through the SharePoint site because you need to set Navigation adjustments.

1. Users need to navigate to Site Settings through the Settings drop-down menu.
2. Browse to the Look and Feel section to access the Navigation page that controls arrangements for both the yellow top menu and bright blue quick launch bar.

6. Applying SharePoint Site Usage Reporting

The built-in reports in SharePoint display information about site visitor data and document popularity.

View Site Usage

1. Go to your SharePoint site.
2. Proceed to Site usage through Settings menu by choosing the Settings gear icon.
3. The site displays several pieces of information which include:
   o Total views of the site.

- The most engaged and viewed documents are categorized under Top Content since users tend to attend those documents frequently.
- The website user activity depends on the number of active visitors who explore its content.

Site Activity Reports

Site usage information together with traffic analytics and security events can be found in the usage report section of the Microsoft 365 Administration Center.

7. Managing Site Lifecycle

SharePoint sites can lose their utility during a project execution because their value to the business requirements diminishes or becomes unnecessary. The site's cleanliness along with efficiency depends on proper lifecycle management.

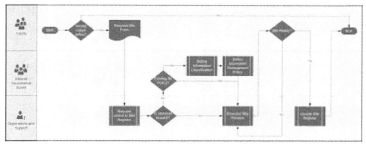

Site Lifecycle Management

Archiving Sites

You should put a site into archival status when it stops being active:

1. Delete whichever is unnecessary in the site.
2. The system updates permissions to keep the document from being changed or distributed.
3. Storing website content in an archive site works best for prolonged periods of storage.

Deleting Sites

When the site becomes unnecessary you need to permanently delete it:

1. From your settings button choose the site settings menu.

2. Under Site Actions at the bottom of populations choose Delete this site to remove the website.

Note: Before deletion download the valuable content on this site since the process is permanent.

8. SharePoint Site Management: Some Guidelines

- **Keep It Simple**: Use content the right way and stay away from putting too much into your site.
- **Regularly Review Permissions**: Users need to have permission to access only what they need to support their work.
- **Use Metadata**: Adding metadata to documents allows easy document search for users.
- **Maintain Version Control**: Utilize SharePoint version tracking to find out who modified documents and restore past document versions if required.
- **Monitor Site Usage**: Check site data every day and week to see if users work with content in the right way and possibly adjust functionality.

Conclusion

To set up and use SharePoint sites in Microsoft 365 is much better than any other communication and documents organization in the practically in practical teams that we have now. I agree with optimizing, with the user experience on the site by using the site features and following best practices in how to lay content and manage access to the site. No matter if you are a small team leader, project manager or head of the organization, SharePoint provides you with the ability to organize your work, your team and your content.

Microsoft SharePoint's Document Libraries

SharePoint Document Library is a customized site that helps you to store and catalog files for a team or organization. This helps in managing the documents, organizing version as well as provide a secure way to share the same document. SharePoint relies on these libraries, they are core to the functionality of the file sharing, and are popular general repositories for a wide variety of files, including traditional office documents as well multimedia, and even PDF.

1. What is a Document Library?

One of the features one can add in a SharePoint sites is a Document Library which is hereby a secure site for documentation. They can upload some of their documents and folders and access rights to other documents with people. Most often, libraries are the fundamental bricks utilized in the quest of document management and retention through a SharePoint site.

2. Creating a Document Library

Creating a new Document Library in SharePoint can be done by:

1. **Go to Your SharePoint Site**:
   o To do that, follow these steps: Go to your SharePoint site to where you would like to create the document library.

2. **Create a Library**:
   o Go at the top of the web page, click the Settings gear and select Site contents.
   o Click New > Document Library.

3. **Set Library Details**:
   o Your instruction is to name the particular library you would create, for instance, "Project Documents" or "Marketing Files".

o The admin can decide whether the library can be placed in the sitemaps navigation and provides an optional description to be given to the libraries.

4. **Create the Library**:

   o Using the above settings (or similar), once you have attaining them, you head over to create to develop the very library you need.

3. Document Library Features

a. Uploading and Storing Files

- **Upload Files/Folders**: Documents can be uploaded via dragging, dropping the documents in the library or a separate 'upload button' which takes the user to his computer's library.

- **Multiple File Uploads**: The great advantage which this tool has is that it can upload lots of files at a time (or even a whole folder).

SharePoint Document Library

b. Organizing Files and Folders

- **Folders**: Similarly, document libraries can create document navigation folders in case if they want to. The folder helps in the creation of the sub compromising so that the files can be categorized in a structure manner.

- **Metadata**: Apart from this, • It will be easy for you to search and manage your documents if you apply metadata on them such as tags, categories, dates. etc SharePoint has the ability to define new attributes on the document for each distinct type of the document.

c. Documents and document versions

- **Versioning**: It has also struck me that it is possible-save and version changes in documents using SharePoint. In addition, documents saved in SharePoints have a record of version history in its background and previously maintained file version, so that its user can go back to the previous file in the event of data loss.

- **Version Control Settings**: The program offers users the following version control parameters:
  - Each significant version update at 1.0 or 2.0 should stay independent from other versions.
  - The system should store every version from major to minor (includes drafts in addition to revised documents).
  - The number of versions should remain limited since an excessive collection enlarges the library size.

d. Check-In/Check-Out

- **Check-Out**: The check-out function makes a document inaccessible to others for editing thus preventing simultaneous editing of your work. The feature becomes essential for documents which need multiple review approvals by different stakeholders.

- **Check-In**: The system becomes accessible for other users after returning a document to its archive following completion of editing through Check-In. Users can submit notes regarding changes when they perform the system check-in operation.

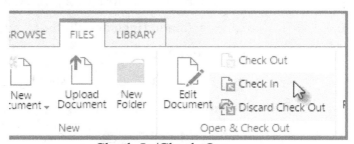

Check-In/Check-Out

4. Permission management in Document Libraries

SharePoint document libraries function with permissions to control access and modifying rights and sharing capabilities for all files in the collection.

a. Setting Permissions

- **Library Permissions**: The system enables users to set access rights for entire document library permissions. SharePoint allows permissions to be assigned at both user-specific and inclusive user types (such as Owners, Members and Visitors).

- **Item-Level Permissions**: A user can apply permissions at both the item and folder level within the document library. Document safety becomes more practical by using this method especially when protecting sensitive information such as bank details.

b. Inheriting Permissions

By default document libraries obtain their permissions from the site they reside in. The inheritance of permissions can be stopped allowing you to apply designated permissions to libraries or documents.

To manage permissions:
1. Go to the Library Settings.
2. Below Permissions and Management, select Permissions for this document library.

3. Versions of the file that you do not want to inherit permissions from should have their permissions stopped through the Stop Inheriting Permissions selection.

5. Document Library Views

The SharePoint SubWebsites system provides users with document formatting tools to achieve their required view configuration. The owner can establish custom views within the document library through proper filtering techniques and metadata sorting and column selection.

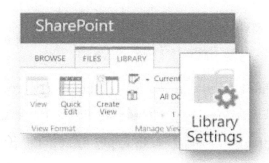

Document Library Views

a. Standard Views

- **All Documents**: The search retrieves all documents present inside of the library.

114

- **List View**: The available List View contains multiple options including □ General view: a list of documents with file name, date of modification, and author's name.
- **Tile View**: The Tile View displays files through big icons which work best for image viewing.

b. Custom Views

- A document sorting process can be created with multiple distinct perspectives using metadata evaluation such as status and department fields. Users can build document views which display either approved documents or documents linked to particular projects.
- **Column Filters**: The system enables users to reduce search results using Column Filters through document properties such as date and author information and metadata.
- **Grouping**: Metadata tools such as project title or document kind should be utilized to create organized groups.

c. Setting Default Views

- The document library needs control modification to display documents without user metadata present. When users access the library for the first time they will encounter the home view as their main screen.

6. Other features include collaboration features in document libraries

a. Co-Authoring

Horizontally collaborative co-authoring functions exist in SharePoint because multiple team members can edit the same document simultaneously. All modifications made by users become instantly visible to other members of the system at the same time.

- Microsoft Word and Excel and PowerPoint and Office Online together with their application versions (Excel Online and Word Online) enable users to co-author files.

b. Alerts

Irrespective of what happens to documents you need to create alerts in the document library to obtain notification about modifications and additions and deletions. The system provides email and text message alerting features for notifications.

To set up an alert:

1. Go to the document lbrary.
2. Select the documents or folder that need monitoring from the available options.
3. The desired alerts should be selected from the Alert Me options which can be located in the same ribbon.

7. Sharing and Synchronizing Files

a. Sharing Documents from the Document Library

The Share button located in the library allows users to give personal access to documents for everyone. Through this system users obtain multiple permissions control for documents that enable either read-only viewing or full editing.

- **Share with internal users**: Document distribution between organizational personnel or project collaborators takes place under the category of internal document sharing.
- **Share externally**: The Share function lets external individuals know about files when admin settings permit such sharing.

b. Sync Files with OneDrive

Users can achieve SharePoint document library file synchronization through the OneDrive sync client installation on their local computer. Through this functionality you will be able to work offline on files then your changes will sync back when your system establishes an Internet connection.

1. To start synchronization choose the sync function at the document library.
2. Sign in with the Microsoft 365 account credentials.
3. Files located in the document library will create a corresponding folder on your PC or MAC system.

8. File Management and Security

a. Retention Policies

Retention policies placed on documents should specify for how long the documents in the library shall be kept. For example you can set the policy that certain files are deleted or moved to archive if some specific number of days passes on the files that resides in document library so as to avoid violating your compliance.

b. Content Types

Define content types to manage the operations of picking documents into the library. Content type is a form of abstraction which might be the description of the columns, workflow at this content type and it needs to have certain policies.

9. Document Library Best Practices

To document SharePoint efficiently, follow these best practices:

- **Keep the Library Organized**: It is required for establishing clear titles for directories and documents as well as the metadata.

119

- **Limit Folder Depth**: Because nested folders are typically elaborate and consequently end up applying a cascade effect on the links, and that is able to make website navigation complicated. However, instead of a metadata and view-based solution to manage documents, use a solution.

- **Use Document Set**: Multiple documents can be collected together by the document set and for that becomes easier to deal with all these documents as one.

- **Enable Version Control**: It always makes sense for enabling document versioning—especially when it comes to vital documents so as to keep track of various versions and record that of prior versions.

- **Monitor Permissions**: Always check some of the individuals that are delegated to have access to the document library then make appropriate changes.

- **Use Views for Efficiency**: Store and manage unique views per folder that allow the most used documents be easily located based on specific parameters – status, date and author for instance.

Conclusion

Document Libraries is one of the basic site features within SharePoint and also an efficient means of organizing files and sharing between the teams and organization. It also provides clear and secure locations in which records can be readily stored and retrieved as well as uploading of documents for sharing. In this paper, SharePoint document library features along with document versioning, co-editing, metadata, and permissions are outlined in brief and their use in managing content and collaboration is explained.

Collaborating with Microsoft Teams

Microsoft Teams is comprehensive communication software that helps enhance team collaboration in small teams via conversation, scheduling, documentation, and integration with other software at businesses. At the same time you are planning to work with your coworkers or dealing with external partners, Microsoft Teams is the key for communication, and business processes.

Here is an overview on how to cooperate successfully with Microsoft Teams:

1. Setting Up Teams and Channels

Teams and channels are the two fundamental elements of Microsoft Teams. A Team is usually a Group Conversation among users working on a common objective while a Channel is a space for a specific discovery in a Team.

Creating a Team

To create a Team:

1. Open Microsoft Teams.
2. Launch the software and find the symbol for Teams in the left-hand side panel.
3. Select Join or go to the bottom and make a team.
4. Select Create team.
5. Choose from:
   - Greenfield (create a project team from very first step.
   - From one or even multiple offices 365 groups that have already existed and is already associated to one groups that uses one group.
6. Admit it and give it a brief description enterprise sure to set your settings through either.

7. To invite contact to the team just insert email address of the participant or choose it in your contact list.

Creating Channels

- **General Channel**: This is the general channel for any group, used for team announcement or other general topic.
- **Additional Channels**: they can create many specific channels from multiple discussion to project channel, topic channel, department channel.

To create a new channel:

1. In the app interface, go to the team to which you wish to apply the channel.
2. Click to the right of the team's name to the three dots (more options).
3. Select Add channel.
4. Name the channel and change the privacy on the channel.
5. Click Create.

2. Chat and Messaging in Teams

The Teams Chat is able to perform such functions as sending quick messages to other users, transferring files. People in The Platform they can use chat to communicate one-to-one, in a group, or in a new way, a Channel.

Start a Chat

1. To the left side bar, navigate to the Chat Section.
2. New messages are displayed as an envelope icon and are separated by the sender – click on New Chat (pencil).
3. To initiate a conversation with that particular individual, include his/her/their name and start typing your message.

Group Chats

- Also, you can create group chat for team and everyone can join into the chat at the same time where you can add the files, task and notes.
- Group chat has features of sending docs gifs and mentions that notifies a specific person.

Chat and Messaging in Teams

Threaded Conversations in Channels

- Once you send a message in a channel, the entire channel conversation is categorized, and as such, whenever individuals reply to your message, they are actually extending the conversation one level further down in what we can refer to as sub-conversations that do not re-populate the main feed. This leads to successful communication and an easy flow of communication to enable that the objectives of the company is achieved.

3. File Sharing and Collaboration

One other benefit that can be attributed to the company is file sharing which is tightly coupled to OneDrive and SharePoint.

Sharing Files in Teams

1. In chat or channel go to the right corner options menu and select the Attach (paper clip option).
2. Select a file on your computer or a file in OneDrive or SharePoint.
3. Anyone that is in a conversation or Channel of the file will be able to look at the file; make comments, find work it.

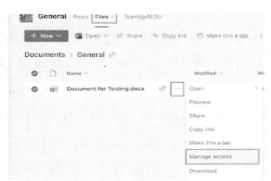

Sharing Files in Teams

Co-Authoring Documents

- Of all the features of Teams, there is the one that allows users to collaborate when editing Office documents – Word, Excel, and PowerPoint using co-authoring. As the features are incorporated into the project, multiple users' edit applies changes

126

simultaneously and the changes are visible to all users.

Document Collaboration Tools

- **Version History**: Version History Files stored in OneDrive in Teams have version history in SharePoint – so when necessary you can always get to any prior versions of documents.
- **Commenting**: Users can provide comments where & how it is needed right within the document without having to come out of another interface.

4. MBR: Meetings and Video Conferencing

Users of Teams can arrange meetings and video conferencing and has got the two into one interface.

Scheduling a Meeting

1. Click on the left side and select Calendar.
2. Press on new meeting or meet now (conference meetings).
3. Revitalize the meeting details (name, time, address, and attendee).
4. Click Send to send the meeting and calendars the date of the meeting.

Joining a Meeting

- If it's your scheduled meeting, you'll find it in the Calendar section, and if it was launched in a Teams channel, you can also click to access it from there.

Meeting Features

- **Screen Sharing**: Share your screen or a specific window during the meeting to other meeting attendees.
- **Recording**: With Teams, you'll be able to record meetings and have them available to search for at a later time.
- **Background Effects**: You don't need to be surrounded by poster, books, clothes etc. because you can blur the background or even replace it while video call.
- **Live Captions and Subtitles**: These enhance inclusivity of meetings and deliver a live subtitles in meeting.

5. Full integration with Microsoft 365 applications

Teams is closely integrated with other Microsoft 365 programs like Word, Excel, PowerPoint, Planner, Teams, Outlook, and more for maximize teamwork.

Using Office Apps in Teams

- **Word, Excel, PowerPoint**: Microsoft office files can be looked at and edited in teams with no moving over to different applications. TEAMS support co-authoring of documents.

Planner Integration

- With Microsoft Planner it is possible join to Teams allowing individuals can collaborate tasks, allocating various duties in a channel. Each of the tasks can be configured to have a deadline as well as its priority and the following ownership.

Outlook Integration

- It means that Teams integrates with Outlook, which this way you are able to tentatively schedule meetings, monitor emails, and also view the Outlook calendar all out of this application.

6. Task and Project Management

Thanks to integration with Planner and Todo, the handling of the tasks and projects in Teams, therefore, remain uncomplicated.

Tasks in Teams

1. **Planner**: Planner enables teams to follow through on work based on tasks, deadlines and completion. You can set goals as well as add errands and work; it is possible also to assign tasks to other staff and analyses outcomes.

2. **To-Do**: Microsoft To-Do can integrate with Teams and you can manage personal tasks, and then also team collaboration tasks.

Task Management Features

- **Assignments**: Tasks can be made and suggested to a user with due date and priority.

- **Progress Tracking**: There is an extra field on the task board to monitor the process of something, what can be not started, ongoing or completed.

7. Collaboration Tools in Teams Channels

Channels allow each discussion to be particular, helping organizations with all a speech to an specific organization added under same channel. In these channels it can be integrated several tools of collaboration with which can be made communications and exchanges of materials.

Use of Tabs

- Tabs within the channels of Teams also allow you to mash up much like is already needed in MS 365 such as document libraries, SharePoint, Power BI reports or even Third party apps.

Wiki in Teams

- Each channel has a Wiki section which is the place for you to add notes or procedures and upload files with. It is also good for keep track of various concepts, events or reference materials in convenient upping of notebook.

8. Teams Security and Compliance

Microsoft Teams works with enterprise security and compliance needs as its template.

Data Security

- **Encryption**: All Microsoft Teams communication data sent and stored is protected using the most advanced encryption methods.
- **Multi-Factor Authentication (MFA)**: Teams has support for MFA for greater account security.

Compliance

- Teams adhere to industry regulations for GDPR, HIPAA and SOC 2 — guaranteeing your correspondences and information storage complies with legal and regulatory necessities.

9. Tips, Strategies, and Techniques of Working Efficiently in Teams

To get the most out of Microsoft Teams, here are some tips for best use:

1. **Keep Channels Focused**: Do group work on one single subject areas, activities, or department of business. All this saves a lot of time and keeps all the messages organized, so all those, who requires some type of information, will be aware where you can get it.

2. **Use @mentions**: When tagging particular individuals, they will not lose sight of key posts that others may expect them to respond.

3. **Set Clear Guidelines**: Determine the standards for reporting, collecting, collaboration and dissemination that matters in large groups. By way of example, decide on when to use chats versus

when to use channels when deciding which kinds of discussions to opt for.

4. **Utilize Tasks**: For the tasks and tasks, use Planner and To-Do in order to reach all the due dates.

5. **Make Use of Files**: Files icon in each of the channel to share and work on the files. Documents should be rev, if possible, and co-authoring should be included to increase productivity.

Conclusion

Microsoft teams is an application whose purpose is to improve communication and collaboration with team within the company for the file sharing meeting project management. It provides the opportunity therefore the partnership can be enhanced by teams and channels, document work can be done, and the superb set of integrated Microsoft 365 tool class. When you combine it with principles of communication and project management, Teams offers the assemblage for high performance work from your team as never Baja.

CHAPTER FOUR

CONCLUSION

Recap of Microsoft 365 Tools

Microsoft 365 is a service that gives you one answer to exactly how to operate efficiently, tweak and generate documentation and messages, exchange ideas and collaborate and also program occasions. Here is a quick rundown or a summary of the major tools found in Microsoft 365, along with their key features:

1. Microsoft Word

- **Purpose**: Preparing and editing text reports and other reports similar in form.
- **Key Features**:
    - Advanced formatting options
    - Technologies to permit team work with the ability to make all edits simultaneously.
    - Templates and design tools
    - Client information systems allowing us to work together even with the ability of instant changes.
    - Read screen content, speak text, closed caption, context analysis, draw shapes, spell, show websites, pop-up definition.

2. Microsoft Excel

- **Purpose**: Sorting data, data organizing, and excel document preparation.
- **Key Features**:
    - Many numbers, formulas, works and functions for Licensing, Police, Bluelight, Traffic, Compute and Timers, complicated calculations etc.
    - The chosen data are to be processed with the aid of PivotTables, in order to draw the graphical representation of the charts.
    - Data analysis tools like Power query and Power Pivot.
    - Immediate sharing and collaboration on the same document
    - Integration for Power BI for further analysis.

3. Microsoft PowerPoint

- **Purpose**: Creating presentations.
- **Key Features**:
    - To Select of templates that includes lots of the options of design whereby the use of templates and themes is involved.
    - Transitions for moving from the current content to & selected other displays.

135

- o Integration with Teams for live presentation.
- o Code editor integration tools with editing options for the team.
- o The other method is the presenter mode with notes and the timer.

4. Microsoft Outlook

- **Purpose**: E mail calenderer and contract, task list.
- **Key Features**:
  - o Email and calendar management
  - o Invitation to schedule and meetings
  - o Task and to-do list management
  - o Integration with Teams and OneDrive
  - o Focused Inbox para separar e-mails import antes

5. Microsoft OneDrive

- **Purpose**: Document management, storing of data, file sharing.
- **Key Features**:
  - o It is primarily focused on store, share and synchronization of files in user interactive way.
  - o Co-authoring of documents
  - o File versioning and history

- Office apps compatibility for smooth working.
- Security features such as file security feature

6. Microsoft Teams

- **Purpose**: Integrated Open forum and Co-operative Media.
- **Key Features**:
  - Chat, voice, and video calls
  - Share of files and collaboration within channels
  - One other feature that is wonderful regarding the utilization of G suite is the option to rapidly integrate with Office apps and OneDrive.
  - Project management teams and collaboration teams
  - Meeting scheduling/ Live events

7. Microsoft SharePoint

- **Purpose**: Business document control and sharing solution.
- **Key Features**:
  - Construct, upkeep, and create worldwide websites for a variety of kinds of teams.

- Document repositories for most file storage
- Automated and personalized JavaScript
- Communication through Intranet sites layout
- Security and permission and access control

8. Microsoft Planner

- **Purpose**: A purpose assignment and project tracking software.
- **Key Features**:
  - The generation of tasks, track them through the process and assigning these tasks.
  - Wall hooks adhering to the philosophy of Kanban boards
  - Integration with Microsoft Teams and Microsoft Outlook
  - A date of completion of tasks, list of tasks and task files
  - Notification and status updates

9. Microsoft OneNote

- **Purpose**: Note-taking and organization.
- **Key Features**:
  - Take the notebooks, sections and pages to gather the information joined with colleagues of the group.

138

- Sharing of notes with other members of a particular working group.
- Handwriting and drawing support
- Marker for identification for simple search and retrieval
- Outlook and other applications of the Office suite

10. Microsoft Power Automate

- **Purpose**: Diminish repletion work and the measure of how much can be finished through autonomous procedures.
- **Key Features**:
  - See some examples of bot check-in data, data input and request for approvals
  - Interoperability with other applications in Office family, SharePoint and Google Workspace.
  - Listen, execute an action on an event (e.g. have received mails).
  - Desktop no-code graphical interface in order to develop and make the workflows.
  - Standard scenarios, that most people would want to automate

11. Microsoft Power BI

- **Purpose**: Business Analytics as well as insights and data presentation.
- **Key Features**:
  - Design colorful presentations of data in reports and boards
  - Access numerous sources of information (MS Excel, databases, web)
  - Providing information and being relatives with peasants
  - Real-time data updates
  - Artificial intelligence data analysis and trends

12. Microsoft Forms

- **Purpose**: Create surveys, questions and quizzes and polls.
- **Key Features**:
  - Quite simple creation of forms that contain questions and can be modified based on end-users preferences.
  - Automated response collection and later analysis in the hands of a live campaign.
  - Linking this apparatus with excel for data analysis

140

- Custom themes and branding for forms
- Collaborative form creation

13. Microsoft Bookings

- **Purpose**: Making appointment and booking meetings.
- **Key Features**:
  - Generally-booked space for end users to book meeting.
  - The integration with the Outlook calendar for the purpose of availability synchronization
  - Notifications and follow-ups
  - Flexible service portfolio and accessibility of the employees
  - Access that requires use of a Microsoft account username and password

14. Microsoft Visio

- **Purpose**: Instruction, rehearsing and reflection activities: diagramming.
- **Key Features**:
  - Draw the whole systems, process, computer, and human relationship in the form of

flowcharts, network diagrams, and the organizations charts.

- o Connectivity to the Microsoft apps such as Excel and SharePoint
- o Cooperation features to exchange and modify diagrams
- o Templates for common diagram types
- o Interconnected to be accessible from any place

15. Microsoft Stream

- **Purpose**: Video management and sharing.
- **Key Features**:
  - o Upload, sharing and show video? Safely
  - o Enclosed video Captions and subtitles for access
  - o supported Adding into Teams for taking meetings
  - o Metrics or analysitsts to count viewings of the videos and level of interaction.
  - o It's always a possibility for shared within the company is selected for a private to give some employees access of the site of a other big companies.

16. Microsoft Delve

- **Purpose**: Quick view of personal information and ability to share that content and work on it.
- **Key Features**:
  - Remove and classify documents from Microsoft 365
  - Dynamic content filtering based on the activities
  - It is completely integrated with OneDrive, SharePoint and Teams.
  - Document stored and shared by users and visible by other organization members
  - Based information around your location and actions

17. Microsoft Sway

- **Purpose**: Lessons also teach her how to create and publish interactive reports, presentations and e-mail newsletters.
- **Key Features**:
  - How it is functional, convenient and user-friendly because of the straightforwardness of the drag and drop method of creating content.

- Integrating with other media such as picture, clip, and voice.
- Publish as an embed link or add it to any other web page
- The application has such navigation features as, clickable navigation
- Online for they are accessible and distributable of data from the cloud.

18. Microsoft to Do

- **Purpose**: Time management and company over view.
- **Key Features**:
  - Use due dates in those lists to plan and track tasks
  - Sync tasks across all devices
  - Organization: classify work in terms of importance
  - Microsoft Outlook integration in terms of task management
  - Categorize and subdivide task lists for other end users, so that a certain list can currently be worked on by many of the users.

19. Microsoft Whiteboard

- **Purpose**: A collaborative and idea generation platform.
- **Key Features**:
    - Join and work, build and participate in interactive whiteboards
    - You are able to work closely with your colleagues on the process of developing a course of action.
    - Include shapes, post-it, and annotations on whiteboards
    - Work with teams for online meeting
    - Synchronize with a cloud from anywhere of any device.

Conclusion

Microsoft 365 is a fantastic set of applications that enable people to work efficiently, collaborate, distribute data, and store information. Whether you are composing with Word, analyzing information with Excel, handling team work via Teams and Planner, or utilizing it with Power Automate, Microsoft 365 is composed from several applications which is offering a single package for individuals or organizational groups.

Efficient Productivity Guide for Microsoft 365

Microsoft 365 is one of the most effective suites that can help people produce more effectively and protect their data, but there are presets that will facilitate to optimize it to the highest possible degree. Refer to the article below to learn more about the list of guidelines that can be used to increase the benefits of using Microsoft 365.

1. Organize Files and Folders Effectively

- **Use OneDrive and SharePoint for Cloud Storage**: OneDrive: Work and resell user files, SharePoint: Group/ project files. Thus allows for file to be shared or synced between devices.
- **Structure Folders Clearly**: Virtually structure this sort of folder decidedly, their consequence should allow customers so as to speedily discover argued documents to (e.g. to category, venture, or duty by year). That means it is a great way of averting clutter in the filleting and, hence, in any thoughts of disorganisation with files.

- **Implement Naming Conventions**: Data file is to be named in a well structured manner to facilitate tracking of a particular file. For example, it is advised not to name the files as 'project report' and use the file names like ProjectReport_2024_01_05.
- **Version Control**: If one is working with Office 365 and OneDrive and SharePoint for documents have so files that the current it is not overwritten when change is made on the document.

2. Master Collaboration Tools

- **Use Microsoft Teams for Communication**: All communications are stored in Teams to see the trail of conversations and reduce the amount of e-mail threads. There are always separate sections for teams or projects which will be primarily involved in the discussion.
- **Collaborate in Real-Time**: Co-author Word, Excel as well as PowerPoint content in real time, which allows you to allow numerous individuals to revise document, table, as well as presentation simultaneously.
- **Share Files via Links, Not Attachments**: Instead of resorting to the attachment utilizing the someone the email as a word document, excel or PDF,

utilizing the One Drive or SharePoint links. This allows for a perfectly timed delivery to all the users of the software.

- **Use @mentions in Teams**: Use @mentions to draw the attention of your colleagues to certain messages, taskserals or files in Teams or in the vaten van de e-mail. This makes for quick replies.

3. Automate Repetitive Tasks

- **Leverage Power Automate**: Application Power Automate is nothing but workflow designed to automatically perform tasks such as to collect data and prepare report or even to respond to email. Make it conditional upon events like new email or form submission.

- **Templates**: You can build the automation flow or the templates for questions answer choices and the choice within the Microsoft Forms with the Power Automate templates that are available only in no code.

- **Use Microsoft Bookings**: Optimize your bookings with Bookings. It enables clients or teammates use to schedule a meeting with you according to your Calendar so that the time for arranging clashes is reserved.

4. Maintain Security and Compliance

- **Set Permissions Carefully**: Develop the use of the permission levels when attending to deliver the documents and files in OneDrive, SharePoint, and Teams. To have the control such that the information exposure is only necessary for exposing the information.

- **Enable Multi-Factor Authentication (MFA)**: They should then make multi-factor authentication for all users so that they have to pronounce something at least twice before they can be able to access the Microsoft 365 applications and services.

- **Regularly Review User Access**: Microsoft 365 Admin Center enables you check user permissions and see who entered the essential info. Replace them if you feel it fit any less or wipe all off.

- **Backup Important Files**: For gargantuan loss data in OneDrive and SharePoint, it needs to be restore those files and folders in which you often use.

5. Maximize the Use of Teams

- **Create Teams and Channels for Projects**: Create Teams and Channels for Projects: Set-up proper Teams and Channels in Microsoft Teams based upon your project, team, department or any regional delivery scope. This is good as it keeps the communication straight and easily accessible.

- **Use Task Management Tools**: Usage of Legerage Planner in a way to organize the projects of Teams. Coordinate responsibilities, timelines and accomplishments in a shared manner with the use of time lines and checklists.

- **Integrate Third-Party Apps**: Moreover, you can log on numerous other apps and tools with Teams so that all your work is extracted into one place. For example, Teams enables the integration of Trello, Adobe, and GitHub, and so on.

- **Schedule Meetings with Teams**: Using Teams to schedule and start up a virtual meeting. Send documents, edit simultaneously & track lessons if a need arises in the future.

6. Organize Emails and Calendars

- **Create Folders and Categories in Outlook**: Organize Inbox by Outlook and segment it with folders. Create the filters to assist in sorting of incoming emails into their specific groups.

- **Utilize the Focused Inbox**: Turn on the Focused inbox to organize mails received inside the device and manage only essential emails.

- **Use Outlook Calendar Efficiently**: Schedule calendars, meetings in walking, appointments, and reminders with the help of Outlook Calendar. If you link to calendar to schedule virtual meetings you will get the output of Teams link to the meeting.

7. Improve Productivity with Shortcuts and Tools

- **Use Keyboard Shortcuts**: Familiarize yourself with Microsoft 365 keyboard shortcuts to work on them more efficiently. Just to take an example, try Ctrl + N to go and open a new document in word, or Alt + Q to search Office wide.

- **Use Templates**: Use more than 500 Word, Excel, PowerPoint and Outlook templates to get your various assignments, such as reports and presentations done.

- **Enable Cortana for Productivity**: If you have a Windows 8 laptop or PC, which doubles as the back office for our business then Cortana can provide you with laborsaving aid that involves using voicing your computer or she can schedule appointments for you.

- **Leverage Microsoft MyAnalytics**: Suchlike, get use of MyAnalytics check and know wherever you are most factual not productive suchlike in sovereign gathering or in an e-mail.

8. Keep Software and Systems Updated

- **Update Office Apps Regularly**: Ensure that all of Microsoft 365 apps are regularly updated to realize all that you can from the applications, through unlocking the latest and the advanced features, the security updates, the usual software flaws.

- **Set Automatic Updates**: Allow how the Microsoft 365 apps will be updated and will update itself to the most recent variety without being manually updated.

- **Manage Updates in Admin Center**: For business users, use Microsoft 365 Admin Center to turn on and control the updates of all accounts on the business and verify that all are in a consistent state of being up to date across all apps.

9. Enhance Data Analysis with Excel and Power BI

- **Use PivotTables and Charts in Excel**: Know to manipulate big data using PivotTables and Charts This is good if you need to, in addition to summarise the information you also want to be able to view results in a short while.

152

- **Combine Excel with Power BI**: Get database analysis with Power BI to the present level. Create real time reports and charts to perceive and need better information.
- **Apply Conditional Formatting**: Now tell me you, about how to Apply Conditional Formatting in Excel, so that the display of visual patterns of the data is clearer.

10. Enable Accessibility Features

- **Use Immersive Reader**: Make use of the Immersive Reader in Word and Outlook when reviewing readings, altering font size, line spacing and color.
- **Enable Dictation**: There's Dictation in Word, Inbox and Teams that shows verbal messages in written text allowing for faster writing processes than prior to being implemented by Microsoft.
- **Use Accessibility Checker**: Ensure that your documents and presentations are for all through the accessibility checker in word, PowerPoint, Excel. This tool is designed to assist in the searching and fixing of any accessibility issues.

Conclusion

With the implementation of such best practises, businesses and individuals will be able to make the most of the Microsoft 365 tools in productivity, security and collaboration terms. Hence, get your functionality organized, automate some tasks, work together using real-time services and take care of the security – it is possible to increase efficiency in business and office work.

www.ingramcontent.com/pod-product-compliance
Lightning Source LLC
LaVergne TN
LVHW022348060326
832902LV00022B/4317